CAMPING *and* ORIENTEERING

Michael Jay

Kingfisher Books

Designed and produced by:
David Jefferis

Edited by:
Jackie Gaff

Illustrated by:
Rhoda and Robert Burns
James Robins
Michael Roffe

Photographs supplied by:
British Orienteering
 Federation
John Cleare
David Jefferis
Rod Organ/Sporting Images
The Scout Association
B Ward
ZEFA

With special thanks to
Black's Camping Shop, London,
for supplying equipment to
be photographed.

Kingfisher Books, Grisewood & Dempsey Ltd,
Elsley House, 24–30 Great Titchfield Street,
London W1P 7AD.

First published in 1990 by Kingfisher Books

Copyright © Grisewood & Dempsey Ltd 1990

BRITISH LIBRARY CATALOGUING IN PUBLICATION DATA
Jay, Michael
    Camping and Orienteering.
    1. Outdoor life – Manuals
    I. Series
    796.5
ISBN 0 86272 414 7

Phototypeset by Southern Positives and Negatives (SPAN),
Lingfield, Surrey
Printed in Spain

Contents

The great outdoors

■ There are few better ways to discover the world of nature than by taking a camping holiday. As well as the daytime adventures of exploring the countryside, there's the excitement of sleeping under canvas or even the stars. Never camp alone, though. Besides being safer if you have an accident or get lost, sharing your trip with friends will add to your fun.

Your holiday will also be safer and more enjoyable if you take time to prepare for it carefully, choosing the correct equipment and improving your map-reading and survival skills.

▶ Most people's idea of a perfect camping holiday includes beautiful weather and spectacular scenery. It's always wise to be prepared for the worst as well as the best, though. Armed with the correct equipment, you'll have a good time whether it rains or shines.

▶ There are lots of different ways to go camping. Although you'll cover more distance on wheels than on foot, without a special mountain bike you'll be limited to tarmac roads.

If you're planning to keep on the move, make sure you travel light. A way of avoiding the weight problem is to choose one site as a base camp for day trips. This is called a 'standing camp'.

Night life

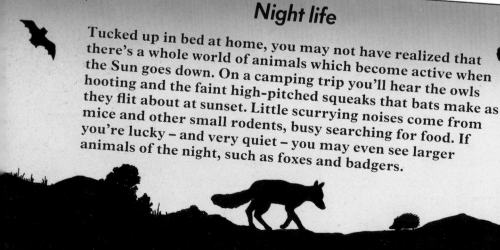

Tucked up in bed at home, you may not have realized that there's a whole world of animals which become active when the Sun goes down. On a camping trip you'll hear the owls hooting and the faint high-pitched squeaks that bats make as they flit about at sunset. Little scurrying noises come from mice and other small rodents, busy searching for food. If you're lucky – and very quiet – you may even see larger animals of the night, such as foxes and badgers.

Prepare for adventure!

■ Good equipment is essential for any camping trip, and lightweight items will take the hard work out of walking with a pack on your back. Make sure you don't carry things you won't really need on the trip.

Most large towns have specialist camping stores – ring and ask about catalogues if you live too far away to visit. Enquire about renting equipment if you don't want to buy the bigger items, such as tents or sleeping bags.

Pack clothes for rain and sun, cold and heat. A short rainproof and windproof jacket with a hood is essential. Wear layers of clothes against the cold, such as long johns or tights under your jeans.

Footwear is very important, and you should always wear in new shoes before you set off. Take proper walking boots, or sturdy shoes with contoured soles – smooth soles are slippery on wet ground. If you plan to walk far in wellingtons, put on an extra pair of thick socks to protect your feet from blistering.

Pack a sunhat for hot weather, and a good sun block cream to protect vulnerable spots such as your nose and the back of your neck.

Simple quilting

Wall quilting

▲ You need to keep warm to sleep properly. A sleeping mat will protect you from the cold ground, as well as cushioning you from bumps and stones. Camping stores sell special mats, but layers of newspaper can do the job more cheaply.

Take a good sleeping bag. Bags filled with down are less bulky than those filled with artificial fibre, but the down bags are more expensive. Look at the quilting, too – wall quilting is the warmest and the best. And check whether the zip is metal or plastic – metal ones feel like ice if you lie against them in the middle of the night!

Backpacks

The best backpacks have a lightweight metal frame with shoulder and waist straps. The frame keeps the bulk of the pack off your back. It also positions the load higher, making it easier to carry.

A badly organized pack will drag around your waist, so put heavy things such as your tent at the top. Breakables should go in the middle. In wet weather, line your backpack with a strong plastic bag and then put your things inside it.

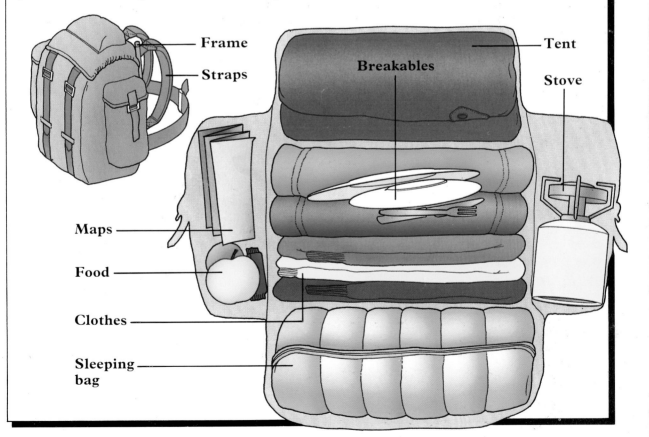

Frame

Straps

Breakables

Tent

Stove

Maps

Food

Clothes

Sleeping bag

Tents

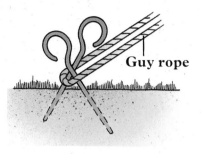

Guy rope

■ The correct tent can make the difference between a disastrous trip and an enjoyable one, so whether you are renting or buying, choose carefully. A simple ridge tent is fine for the occasional summer camping trip, and it is one of the cheapest. Check the weight you'll be carrying on your back as well. With their light alloy poles, many nylon tents big enough for two people weigh less than 3 kilograms.

▲ **Hammer in tent pegs at a 90° angle to the guy rope. On loose soil, hammer in a crossed pair of pegs to keep them in place.**

Tent types

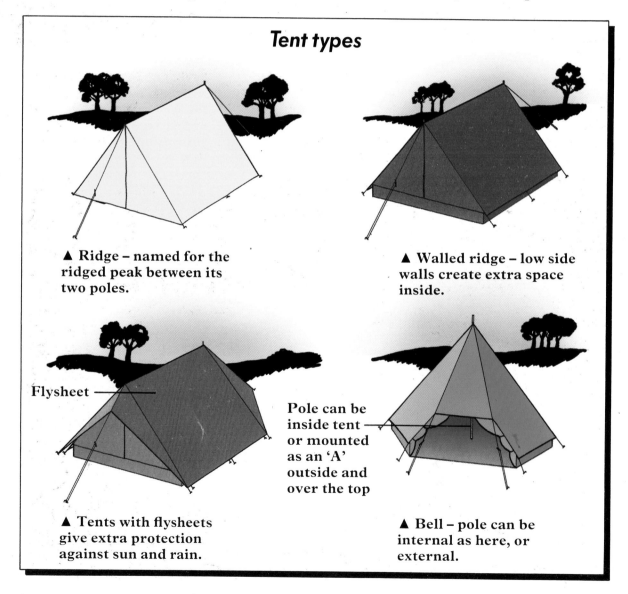

▲ **Ridge – named for the ridged peak between its two poles.**

▲ **Walled ridge – low side walls create extra space inside.**

Flysheet

Pole can be inside tent or mounted as an 'A' outside and over the top

▲ **Tents with flysheets give extra protection against sun and rain.**

▲ **Bell – pole can be internal as here, or external.**

▲ Tents come in a wide range of types, sizes, materials, and prices. These are some of the lightweight nylon tents now available.

▼ Practise putting up your tent at home, *before* you set off on your camping holiday as managing the pegs and guy ropes can be tricky at first. The flysheet goes on last and sits a little above the tent, like an outer roof. Besides keeping off the rain, it keeps the tent cool in sunny weather.

Sleeping under the stars

■ Only sleep out in the open when the weather is really warm. Nights can be cool, even when the days are very hot, so make sure you have a good sleeping bag. Check that there is some sort of shelter nearby, in case it rains and you have to scramble for cover.

Knowing how to erect a temporary shelter, or bivouac, will come in handy if you do get caught in the open when it rains. Below are two examples of quick and easy bivouacs, which you could practise erecting in your garden or (after obtaining permission) in a local park.

▶ **When sleeping in the open, use a groundsheet to stop damp seeping up into your sleeping bag.**

Bivouacs

One way of making a bivouac is to hang a groundsheet over a length of rope tied between two trees, as shown below left. Heavy stones keep the bottom edges of the bivouac in place. Below right is an even simpler version, which uses a wall or a fence for support. This is fine for calm weather, but it should not be used in windy conditions as a strong gust could drag the stones on the wall down on top of you.

Ready to go?

Route	Check that you have all the necessary maps to cover the route you've agreed on with your friends. Contact the local tourist authority for more information. List places you'd like to visit.
Campsites	Mark these on your maps and try to book them in advance, particularly in busy seasons.
Weather	Think of things to do if the weather is bad, and places such as museums you could visit. What games do you play? Playing cards are small and light.
Packing list	Write down everything you can think of, then go through the list again and cross out all the unnecessary items. Find out what the others are taking so that you don't double up – you'll only need one camping stove between you, for instance.
Load sharing	Divide the heavy or awkward items evenly – there is no need for one person to carry the lot!
Contact numbers	Give parents or guardians a copy of your route and phone numbers for the various campsites. Write your name, home address and phone number on a card and keep it on you at all times.
First aid	Your basic kit should include a mild disinfectant to clean cuts and grazes, and a box of sticking-plasters. Take scissors and lint in case you need to bandage a larger wound, and a pair of tweezers for splinters.

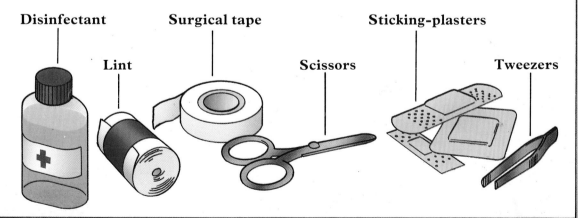

Disinfectant   Surgical tape   Sticking-plasters

Lint   Scissors   Tweezers

Setting up camp

■ Even if you only plan to spend one night at a site, it is well worth taking a little time to choose the best spot for your tent. Look for a dry area which is slightly raised, so that it doesn't get boggy at the first sign of rain. If you can avoid rocks and stones just below the surface, so much the better, as these can make hammering in the pegs a difficult and frustrating experience. Bushes and low trees will give shelter from wind and rain, but don't erect your tent under trees with branches that could snap off in a high wind.

Camping in the wild

You may not always want to stay at a proper site, but if you're planning to camp in the wild, be sure to visit the owner of the land and get permission before you set up camp.

Keep well clear of fields that have livestock in them, and never erect your tent where a crop has been sown.

Check that supplies of fresh water are near to hand before you decide on a site – hiking to get water won't be the most popular of your camping tasks!

▼ Once the camp is set up, you can use it as a base for day trips or watersports such as canoeing.

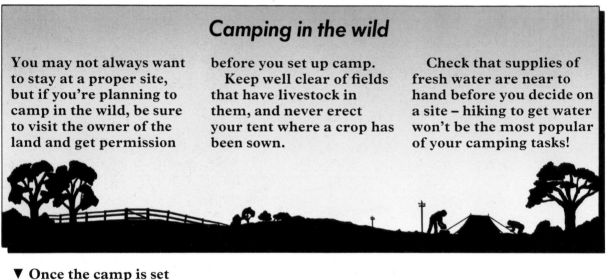

▲ If you're lucky enough to have a good view from your campsite, angle the tent opening towards it.

▲ In windy weather, be extra careful where you position the tent – and the campfire!

▲ Sleeping on a slope isn't easy or comfortable, so try to erect your tent on reasonably level ground.

▲ To avoid discomfort at night, clear the area of pebbles before you put up your tent.

▲ If you're near the sea, don't camp on low-lying ground where the tide might swamp you.

▲ It's handy to be close to a shop or farm where you can buy daily supplies of basic foods.

13

Around the campfire

■ Toasting your toes around a campfire is one of the best ways to end a day in the country, especially if someone has a harmonica or a guitar to get a singsong going. And with a little care and attention, a fire can be as safe as it is enjoyable. Make sure that you collect all the wood you need before it gets too dark to find it, and never cut fresh wood from trees or bushes.

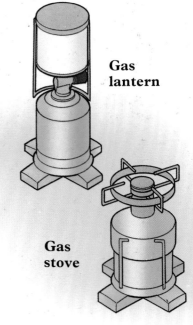

Gas lantern

Gas stove

▶ It isn't always practical to have a campfire, particularly if dry wood is in short supply. A quick and simple alternative is a small camping stove with a disposable gas cylinder.

The latest ones have a built-in sparking system, which lights the gas as soon as you turn it on. Camping-gas lanterns are a good idea for general illumination at night.

Making a campfire

Ask the landowner's permission before collecting wood and lighting a fire and, for your own and others' safety, always follow these simple rules:

☑ Build the fire downwind of your tent, at least 2–3 metres away from it.
☑ The fire shouldn't be near bushes or hedges, or under low boughs of trees.
☑ Clear the area of anything else that might catch alight, especially dry leaves and twigs – the campfire is the only blaze you want going.
☑ Follow the steps below to make a fire without damaging the landscape:

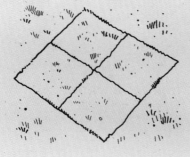

▲ Cut into a 1-metre square area of grass. Divide the square into four quarters.

▲ Roll back the turf and store it upside down in a cool place, ready to be replaced later.

▲ If the fireplace is wet, line it with stones or sand. Make a stone border around the edges.

▲ Nothing tastes quite as delicious as a meal cooked over a campfire!

Douse the fire with water when you've finished with it. When the embers are thoroughly cold and wet, scatter them somewhere out of sight. Remove the stone fireguard and return the stones to where you found them. If you then replace the squares of turf, treading them lightly back into place, there should be little sign left of your fire.

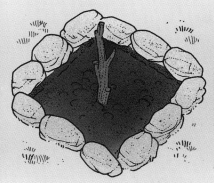

▲ Push a stick into the fireplace, then build a nest of crumpled paper and small sticks.

▲ Light the paper first. When the sticks catch fire, slowly add bigger chunks of dry wood.

▲ Keep adding wood until there is a good blaze going. Watch over the fire at all times.

Outdoor kitchen

■ Rule one for the camp cook is 'keep it simple'. Preparing fussy food isn't easy in a well-equipped kitchen, let alone at a campsite. Rule two is 'keep it clean' – don't get grass or dirt in the food. Rule three is 'cut down on the pots and pans'. As well as being tasty, one-pot meals such as stews will leave your assistants with less washing-up to grumble about!

▼ The campfire kitchen should include the basic utensils shown below. Make sure you take tough equipment that will survive the bumps and thumps of camping – items made of metal or plastic are best as these will not break if they get dropped. The tin opener should be a multi-purpose type which will also open bottles.

► Camping-gas stoves can be used for any cooking which involves boiling or frying. You will get more heat from a stove if you erect a windshield for it, as even a light breeze will blow heat away. Make sure you prop the windshield securely to stop it falling over. The one shown here is specially made for the job.

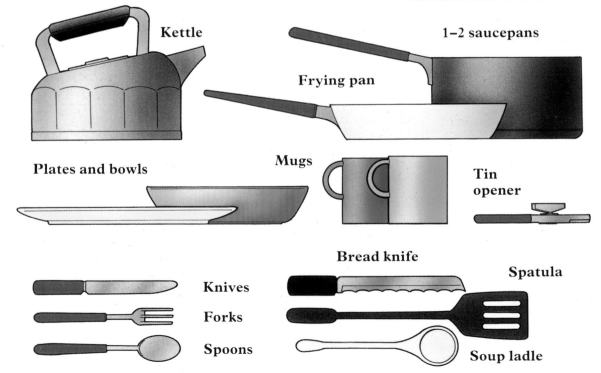

Kettle

Frying pan

1–2 saucepans

Plates and bowls

Mugs

Tin opener

Bread knife

Knives

Forks

Spoons

Spatula

Soup ladle

Eco-sense

☑ Bury vegetable peelings and food waste that will rot in the ground.

☑ Put your other rubbish in a strong plastic bag, ready to be emptied into a site bin or taken with you when you leave.

☑ Be sure to bag up all tins and bottles. Animals or campers could cut themselves on sharp edges, while bright sun focussing through glass could start a fire.

☑ Suspend the rubbish bag well above ground level to stop animals tearing it open and scattering the contents.

☑ Do the washing-up as soon as the meal is over – insects and creepy-crawlies love dirty pots!

Food planning

There's nothing like fresh air for working up an appetite, so make sure you plan a good-sized breakfast and evening meal each day. It's best to take a picnic lunch if you're spending the day away from camp, with chocolate and muesli bars to eat as energy snacks mid-morning and afternoon. Don't forget something to drink! Planning a day's food isn't difficult, and it's a job you can all take turns at doing. Here is a food plan for a weekend trip, to give you a few ideas.

BREAKFAST

Day one

Fruit
Muesli or cereal
Fried egg, with bacon or mushrooms and tomato
Bread fried in pan juices

Day two

Fruit juice
Muesli or cereal
Scrambled eggs on bread, with sausages or mushrooms

LUNCH

Ham or cheese sandwiches, with sauce or pickle
Slice of carrot cake
Yoghurt or fruit

Cheese or peanut butter sandwiches with cucumber or tomato
Slice of flapjack
Yoghurt or fruit

EVENING MEAL

Packet or tinned soup
Barbecued kebabs
Boiled rice
Salad
Packet-mix pancakes with lemon

Grapefruit
Vegetable stew, or meat and vegetable stew
Potatoes wrapped in foil and baked in the camp-fire embers
Tinned peaches and tinned custard

Tying knots

On a camping trip it's a good idea to take along some thin rope or cord – and useful if you know beforehand how to tie proper knots with it. There are dozens of different knots you can learn, but you should find that the four shown here will suit most requirements. Although they may appear rather complicated, with a little practice you'll find them quite easy to master and remember.

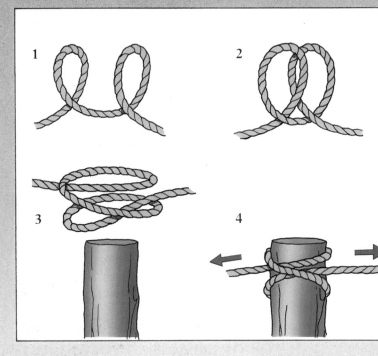

Clove hitch

This knot is used to make non-slip attachments to posts and other solid objects. Fixing a washing line between two trees is just one of the ways a clove hitch will come in handy around the campsite.
1. Make two loops.
2. Place one loop on top of the other.
3. Carefully slip the pair of loops over the top of the post.
4. Pull both ends of the rope to make the knot grip tightly.

Carrick bend

Use this knot to join two ropes. It grips well, but it is also easy to untie.
1. Loop the end of one rope.
2. Lay the second rope over the first.
3. Take the second rope under and between the crossed first rope.
4. Weave the second rope under and through the first loop. Pull the ends of both ropes tightly to finish the knot.

Sack knot

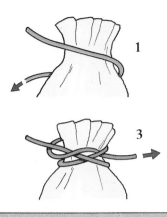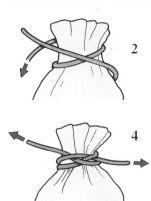

This knot is ideal for keeping animals out of rubbish bags.

1. Loop the neck of the bag.
2. Take one end round to make another loop.
3. Take the end of the second loop over, then under itself.
4. Pull both rope ends to close the bag tightly.

Rope sling

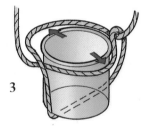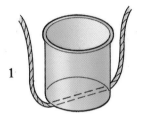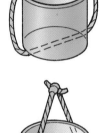

A sling is a very useful way of carrying a container which doesn't have a handle.

1. Centre the container on the rope.
2. Tie the rope ends once across the top.
3. Open one loop, pulling it sideways to make a noose under the lip of the container.
4. Tighten the noose and lift the container.

▼ One way of using a sling knot – to carry water.

Map reading

■ Once you've set up camp, it's time to go exploring. Your best friend now is your map. Use it to plan your route for the day, and remember to take it with you! The time to practise your map-reading skills is *before* you set off though, not when you're out in the wilds on a dark and wet night, not sure where you are . . .

▼ Plan your day's walk carefully and don't try to go too far – an average pace is 3–4 km an hour. Check your map often, to keep on the right track.

A useful map scale is 1:25,000, which means 4 cm of map covers 1 km of land. All natural features are shown, as well as towns, villages and some buildings.

To use a map to find out where you are, begin by looking around you and identifying big features such as hills, forests and villages. When you've found these on the map, look for a smaller feature closer to you, such as a road or bridge. Now line up the map so the features around you match the symbols on it.

▶ The geographical outlines or contours of the land are given on large-scale maps. Contour lines such as those on the right show height above sea level, and measurements are usually given on the lines themselves.

Look at the contour lines when you are planning your walking route, as they show whether land is hilly or flat. The going is steep when the spaces between the contour lines are narrow, while widely spaced contours indicate gentle slopes. And as you can see on the right, you can also identify particular landforms from their contour patterns.

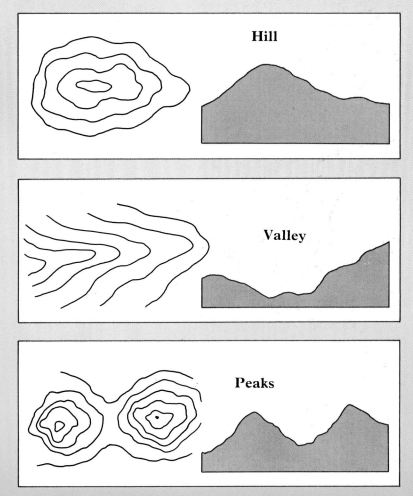

Hill

Valley

Peaks

Sun and star navigation

■ Navigation is the art of finding your way, and it's helped by a good sense of direction and a compass. Below and opposite are some tips on how to navigate without a map or a compass, in case you ever get completely lost. If you choose one direction and stick to it, eventually you'll find a road or a house where you can ask for help. Only head off if you can see where you're going, though. If it is foggy or the night is dark, stay where you are and keep warm until help arrives or the conditions improve.

▶ If you find yourself lost without a compass, you can find your way using the Sun. To do this you need a watch face with hands (for digital watches see below right).

In the northern hemisphere, point the hour hand at the Sun. South is midway between the hour hand and 12 o'clock.

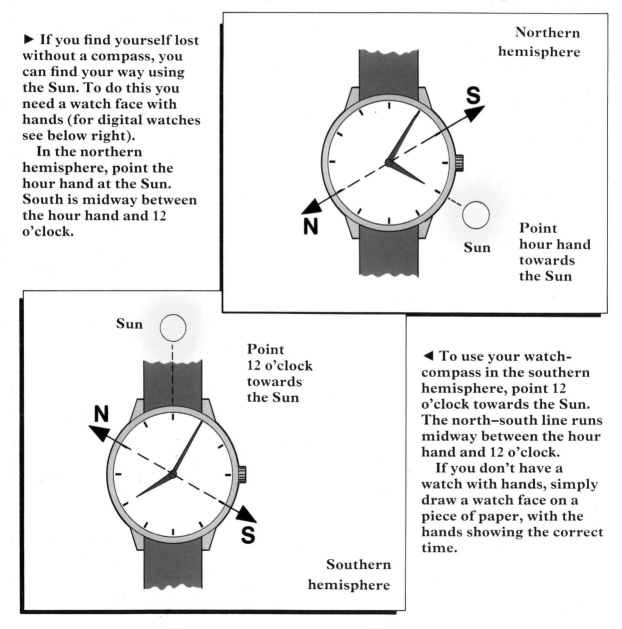

Northern hemisphere

Sun

Point hour hand towards the Sun

Point 12 o'clock towards the Sun

Sun

Southern hemisphere

◀ To use your watch-compass in the southern hemisphere, point 12 o'clock towards the Sun. The north–south line runs midway between the hour hand and 12 o'clock.

If you don't have a watch with hands, simply draw a watch face on a piece of paper, with the hands showing the correct time.

Finding north

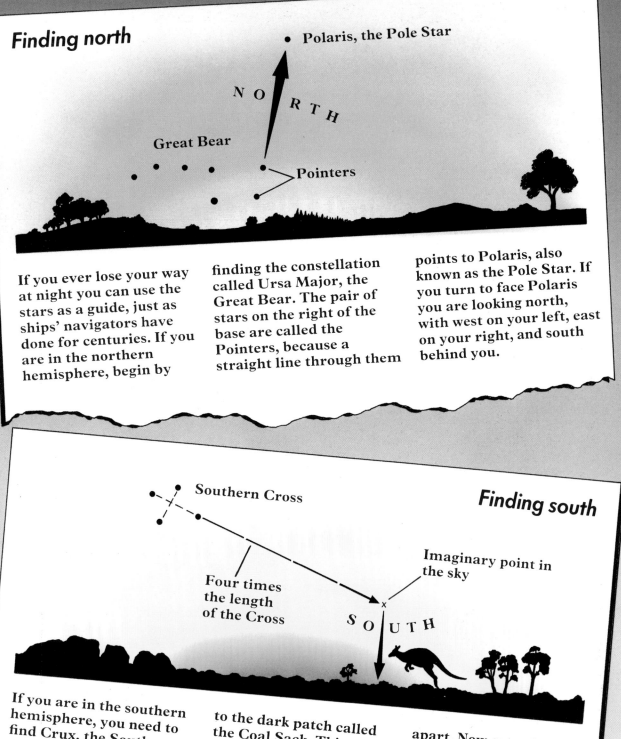

If you ever lose your way at night you can use the stars as a guide, just as ships' navigators have done for centuries. If you are in the northern hemisphere, begin by finding the constellation called Ursa Major, the Great Bear. The pair of stars on the right of the base are called the Pointers, because a straight line through them points to Polaris, also known as the Pole Star. If you turn to face Polaris you are looking north, with west on your left, east on your right, and south behind you.

Finding south

If you are in the southern hemisphere, you need to find Crux, the Southern Cross. It's quite a small constellation, so look along the faint band of the Milky Way until you come to the dark patch called the Coal Sack. This marks the edge of the Southern Cross stars. Make the cross by imagining lines between the two closest stars and the two farthest apart. Now extend one line as shown above, making it four times as deep as the cross. If you face the point at the end of this imaginary line, you are looking due south.

Into the unknown

■ Armed with your map-reading and navigation skills, you're now ready to face the unknown and enjoy it. Even so, telling someone at the campsite your route and when you expect to return is a wise precaution in case you get lost or are injured in some way.

You might like to take a notebook and a small camera or sketchpad with you, to record your journey and any interesting wildlife you may discover.

▶ **A small frameless backpack is ideal for carrying things you'll need during the day. Spare clothes will depend on the weather, but don't forget a rainproof jacket.**

Take a torch and a whistle to signal for help in an emergency – repeat the SOS signal of three short, three long, three short whistle blasts (or torch flashes at night).

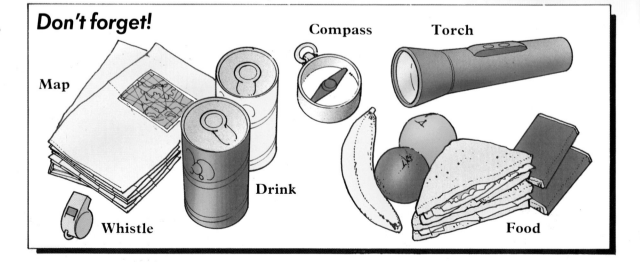

Don't forget!

Map

Whistle

Drink

Compass

Torch

Food

▲ Exploring wild country can be fascinating, but keep an eye on your watch and allow time to get back to camp before nightfall.

The Country Code

Here are some reminders to treat the country with the respect it deserves – enjoy the scenery, but leave it as you found it.

☑ Close gates after you, even if you find them left open.

☑ Don't pick or damage wild flowers or plants.

☑ Be wary of animals, as few like to be approached and some can be dangerous if cornered. Watch out for snakes.

☑ Keep to paths across farmland, and walk around fields if a path isn't clear – even grass is a valuable crop!

☑ Take your rubbish back to camp with you, together with any other bits of litter you come across.

☑ Avoid noise pollution too – leave radios at home or keep the sound down.

Weather watching

■ The weather is always changing, so checking the daily weather forecast can mean the difference between being safe and being sorry.

Most changes in weather take place along fronts. These are the areas, or zones, where a cold air mass meets a warm air mass. The three main types of front are illustrated below – you'll find that learning the front symbols will make the weather maps seen in newspapers and on television a little easier to understand.

Warm front

In a warm front, an advancing mass of warm air slides up and over a retreating mass of cold air. Although warm fronts often produce light rain or snow, clearer skies and a rise in temperature follow their passing.

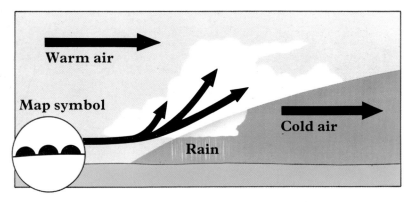

Cold front

This is when an advancing mass of cold air moves under a mass of warm air, forcing it upwards. Cold fronts pass quickly, often producing short, heavy showers. Colder weather follows their passing.

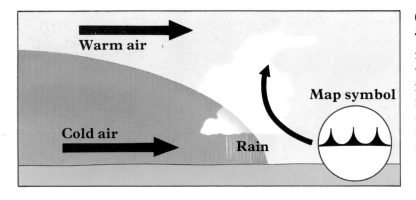

Occluded front

When cold fronts catch up with warm ones, they lift up the warmer air above the Earth's surface. These occluded fronts bring a mixture of cold and warm front weather conditions – heavy, low clouds and long periods of rain or snow.

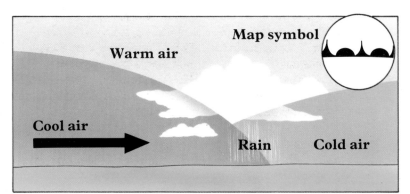

Cloud types

However hard forecasters work at finding out about the weather, there are no guarantees that their predictions will be correct. When you're out in the countryside, recognizing the signs in the sky is just as important a survival technique as being able to read the symbols on a map.

1. **Stratus** – low thick sheets of fog-like cloud, often producing light rain.

2. **Nimbostratus** – shapeless dark-grey cloud, shedding rain in summer and snow in winter.

3. **Stratocumulus** – rolls of light and dark cloud.

4. **Cumulus** – fluffy white cloud seen in fair weather.

5. **Cumulonimbus** – towering mass of dark cloud, giving rain, hail and thunderstorms.

6. **Altostratus** – sheets of pale grey cloud, which can thicken to bring rain.

7. **Altocumulus** – grey streaks and patches of cloud, usually seen in fine settled weather.

8. **Cirrostratus** – high thin haze, which can mean rain or snow is coming.

9. **Cirrocumulus** – small fleecy balls of high cloud, like ripples, often seen before rain or storms.

10. **Cirrus** – thin high cloud often seen when the weather is fine. If curled in 'hooks', rain on the way.

Weather-wise camping

■ Cold, damp, wind and fog are enemies of campers and walkers. But as long as you are well prepared, they needn't cause any great problems. Fog is perhaps the trickiest situation as it is so easy to lose your sense of direction – the sighting-stone method shown on page 29 has been used many times to lead people out of danger. You shouldn't ignore weather signs either, so keep an eye on the sky at all times.

▶ **A lightweight 'space blanket', made of shiny foil, is useful for cold weather emergencies.**

Feet stay snug and warm but don't get sweaty in rubber boots lined with a 'breathing' material.

Defence against wind and rain

Camping in bad weather needs special action. In really high winds, lay heavy rocks over all the tent pegs, after treading the pegs as far into the ground as possible. If camping on a slope in wet weather, dig a shallow ditch on the uphill side above the tent to stop water flooding in.

Drainage ditch

Heavy rock

Danger – fog!

Lay stones behind you, one every few metres

In foggy weather, it's easy to lose your sense of direction and walk in circles. This can be very dangerous in boggy or mountainous country, so stay where you are and keep warm until help arrives or the weather improves. In fairly open country, with even ground, you can hold a course through fog by laying a straight-line trail of stones behind you.

▲ There are lots of folklore sayings which claim to predict the weather. Some of these are quite reliable, such as 'red sky at night, shepherd's delight'. The Sun can only be seen low on the western horizon, reddening the sky, if there is little or no advancing cold front cloud to block our view. That's why fine days usually follow a red evening sky.

Other weather sayings are based on observations of animal behaviour. 'Spiders' webs bigger, weather's going to be better' seems to be true more often than not.

You might like to make a collection of weather sayings, and then test them out on your next camping trip.

Fighting the cold

■ The human body needs to maintain an inside temperature of around 37°C, and people can become very ill if this goes up or down by just a few degrees. That is why keeping warm is your most important survival tactic when the temperature drops. If you plan a camping trip in a country with a very cold climate, the correct protective clothing and equipment are essential.

▶ Canadian winter camping. Inside the tent, sheltered from the bitter winds, campers stay snug and warm. In this time-lapse photograph, stars seem to wheel as streaks of light around the single point of the Pole Star.

The wind-chill factor

Moving air cools bare flesh a lot more quickly than still air – that's why people enjoy a breeze on a hot summer day. Wind is not so pleasant in winter or at night, though. And as the temperature drops and the wind speed increases, wind-chill can become a real menace. Cooled by the wind, flesh temperature can drop below that of the still air, making frostbite a danger. In really cold climates, wind-chill can be a killer.

To prevent loss of body heat, clothing should be wind- and waterproof. Wear lots of layers, because the air trapped between the clothes acts as an insulator, keeping you warm. Fabrics such as wool are best, as they let the skin breathe.

Air temperature °C		10°C	0°C	−10°C	
Wind speed in km/h	8	9	−2	−12	
	16	5	−8	−20	**Wind-chill temperatures**
	32	0	−15	−29	
	64	−3	−21	−36	

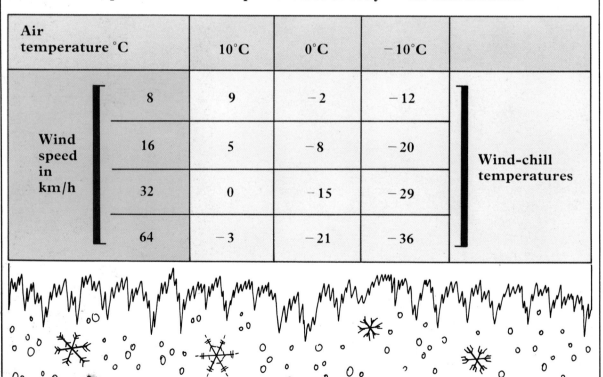

Out in the midday Sun

■ When the weather is hot, one of the ways the body keeps its temperature down is by sweating – the liquid which is evaporated from the skin takes heat with it. If you're planning to walk in the heat, drinking enough to replace the water your body loses by sweating is vital.

Keeping cool so that you don't sweat so much is also important, as is protection against sunburn. Light-coloured clothes are best, as they reflect the Sun's rays. Wear a hat, and use a sun block not a tanning cream. Rest in the shade in the middle of the day, when the Sun is hottest.

▼ The hottest part of the day is when the Sun is high overhead. Here, camel trekkers break at midday for a rest in the shade of some trees. In hot countries, camels make ideal pack animals as they tolerate heat well and can go for weeks on end without food or water.

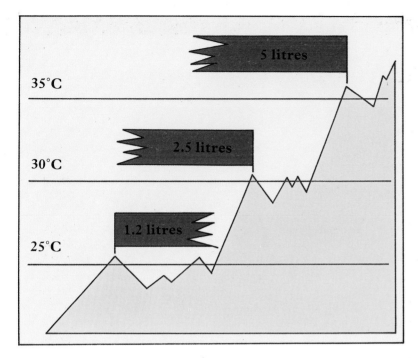

◄ This chart shows the minimum amount of water needed by our bodies each day. The hotter it gets, and the more exercise we do, the more water we need as our bodies lose heat by sweating. Although humans can survive many days without food, they can last only a short while without water.

Protection from the Sun

Clothes are your first line of defence, both in reducing water loss through sweating and in protecting against sunburn. Your head and neck must be covered. If you don't have a hat, use a cloth or spare shirt – and if you've plenty of water, dampening the material will make you cooler.

▲ If you have no sunglasses, you can make eyeshades out of a piece of card, tied at the ends with elastic or string. Cut a pair of eye slits with a knife. Trim off any loose bits of card before you wear the shades.

◄ The French képi protects the back of the neck from the Sun. Make your own képi, using a clean white handkerchief, kept in place by a lightweight sports cap.

A test of map reading and navigation

■ Orienteering is an exciting and competitive sport which will help you to develop your map-reading skills further, while enjoying time out in the countryside. For a typical event, an area is specially mapped and control points are set up within it. Competitors use their map and compass to navigate the quickest way between the various control points.

▼ **The Silva compass was specially developed in Sweden for the sport of orienteering.**

▶ **Suitable clothes for orienteering include a lightweight tracksuit to protect limbs from scratches. There's no need for heavy clothing – running will keep you as warm as toast! Add a pair of comfortable trainers, or special shoes with studs to increase grip on muddy tracks. Take a whistle to summon help in an emergency.**

Carrying cord

Compass needle

Magnifying lens

Sides marked in millimetres and inches

Transparent plastic body can be seen through when laid on map

▲▶ Control points are shown on orienteering maps by numbered circles. On the course, they are identified by red and white buckets or nylon markers.

To prove that they've visited all the control points and haven't cheated, all competitors carry a special card. Each time they reach a control point they use a pin punch to clip a particular area of the card.

Needle punch tied to post

Each control point has a different punch pattern

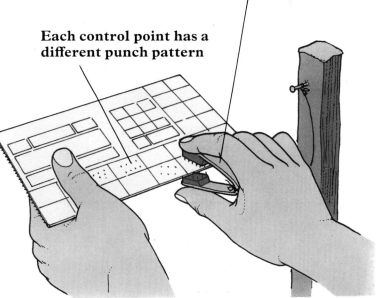

Fastest across the map

Competitors in orienteering events run different routes, depending on their age and skills. So don't follow other people if you get confused – they could be on a different course! Orientate yourself on your map, and if necessary return to a familiar feature and try again.

As well as keeping track of your position on the map, it's important to think of good routes to the next control point. If there's a hill in the way, is it quicker to walk a shorter distance over the top or to run a longer distance around it?

▶ Having studied your map, you need to head for the next control point as quickly as possible. As your 'map memory' improves, you will require fewer stops to check where you are going.

Orienteering events

There are various types of orienteering competition, although the idea behind them remains the same – navigating on the move across unknown country.

Cross-country
This is the most common type of event. Competitors race across a set course, checking in at control points.

Score events
Lots of control points are set up. Each of these has a different score value, and the highest scoring ones are usually farthest from the start line. The winning competitor is the person who collects the highest score within a set time, often one hour.

Relay race
The usual entry is a team of three, each running one third of the course. Unlike most orienteering events, there is a mass start, and the winner is the first to cross the finishing line.

Night orienteering
For night-time events, courses are planned to allow for the fact that competitors will be using torches to find their way. Not a good idea for beginners, but great fun once you are used to daytime competitions.

Line courses
These are usually training events. Competitors are given the line of the course, but not the position of the control points. Following the line will lead you to the control points. If you wander off course, you'll miss them and lose points.

Map memory
This is another training event. The course has to be memorized, one section at a time. Taking part in these events builds up confidence and speed.

Ski orienteering
An event for countries where cross-country skiing is made possible by good snow cover in winter. The rules are much the same as for normal orienteering, but the courses are longer because skis are faster than feet!

▶ This is not quite the rough-country orienteering it looks – in fact, the race is taking place in a wooded city park. But such urban courses give beginners a good introduction to the sport and prepare competitors for the problems involved in navigating out in the wilds. Out in the country, the terrain may be sandy, hilly, wooded slopes or rocky forests. Each course has its own problems and challenges.

Taking pictures

Combining photographs with a diary will make a record of your camping trip much more colourful. Here's some information about the type of photographic equipment that will stand up to the rough and tumble of the walking trail.

Shutter release button

Viewfinder

Electronic flash

Autofocus lens unit

Sliding cover protects lens when not in use

▼ These deer were photographed 'on the hoof' in Yosemite National Park, California. A compact camera is ideal for getting good results from unexpected sights like this.

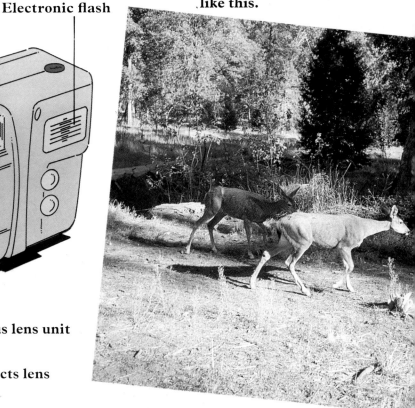

▲ The 'compact' is one of the most useful types of camera. This one has automatic focus, exposure and film wind-on, so it's quick and easy to use. And because it's small and light, it can be carried in a pocket, loaded and ready for action. It also has a built-in electronic flash for low-light and night shots.

Many compact cameras have a sliding cover to protect the lens. Opening the cover switches on the camera.

The more recent models are powered by lithium batteries which have a five-year life. If your camera takes ordinary batteries, make sure you carry a spare set – batteries always seem to

fail at awkward moments.

If you plan on doing water sports such as canoeing, it's worth taking a waterproof camera. These can generally survive a brief dip, and some even float if you drop them overboard. 'Splashproof' cameras can survive rain, but they don't like going for a swim.

Glossary

Bivouac
A temporary camp in the open. Bivouac shelters are simply made from waterproof sheets slung over convenient trees, bushes or low walls.

Breathing materials
General name for those clothing fabrics which keep you warm, whilst letting the natural moisture from your body out. This allows your skin to 'breathe', so you don't get sweaty. A natural breathing fabric is wool. A man-made version is Gore-tex.

Compact camera
General name for pocket-sized automatic cameras.

Control point
One of the stops on an orienteering course. At each control point, competitors use a punch marked with a different pin pattern to record that they have been to the point.

Frame backpack
Rucksack mounted on a sturdy but lightweight metal frame, to which the shoulder and waist harness are attached. Using a frame, the rucksack is kept slightly off the back, which means any lumps in your packload don't dig painful holes in your body. Also, the load stays high up, not slipping to waist level. High-mounted loads are easier to carry.

A frameless backpack is only suitable for light loads.

Groundsheet
Waterproof sheet laid down between a camper and the ground. Its purpose is to stop damp rising from the soil.

Guy ropes
Ropes which keep a tent up.

Képi
Flat cap, with fabric flap at the back to protect the neck from hot Sun. Képis were first used by soldiers in the French Foreign Legion, based in the African Sahara desert.

Map scales
Maps come in various scales according to their use. A popular size for walkers is 1:25,000, or 4 cm to 1 km. Orienteering maps are often scaled to 1:15,000 which allows much more detail to be shown.

Mountain bike
Off-road bicycle equipped with sturdy frame, thick tyres and low gears.

SOS
Emergency 'help' signal, consisting of . . . – – – . . . This dot-dash-dot signal can be made by radio, puffed with smoke, flashed with a torch or even banged on a tin lid. The letters SOS stand for 'Save Our Souls'.

Space blanket
Thin plastic film, covered with a reflective metallic coating. Useful in emergencies as it keeps off wind and retains body heat. Weighs less than 100 grams so can be carried in a pocket.

Standing camp
Campsite used for several days (or even a complete holiday) as a base from which to go out exploring.

Sun block
A cream which can be smoothed onto the skin to prevent burning by the ultra-violet light in sunshine. Small amounts of UV light cause a healthy suntan – too much causes bad skin burns.

Wind-chill factor
Amount by which wind cools a body even more than the temperature of the air. The more wind, the colder you get.

Index